THE TRUE STORY OF MOTHER GOOSE AND HER SON JACK

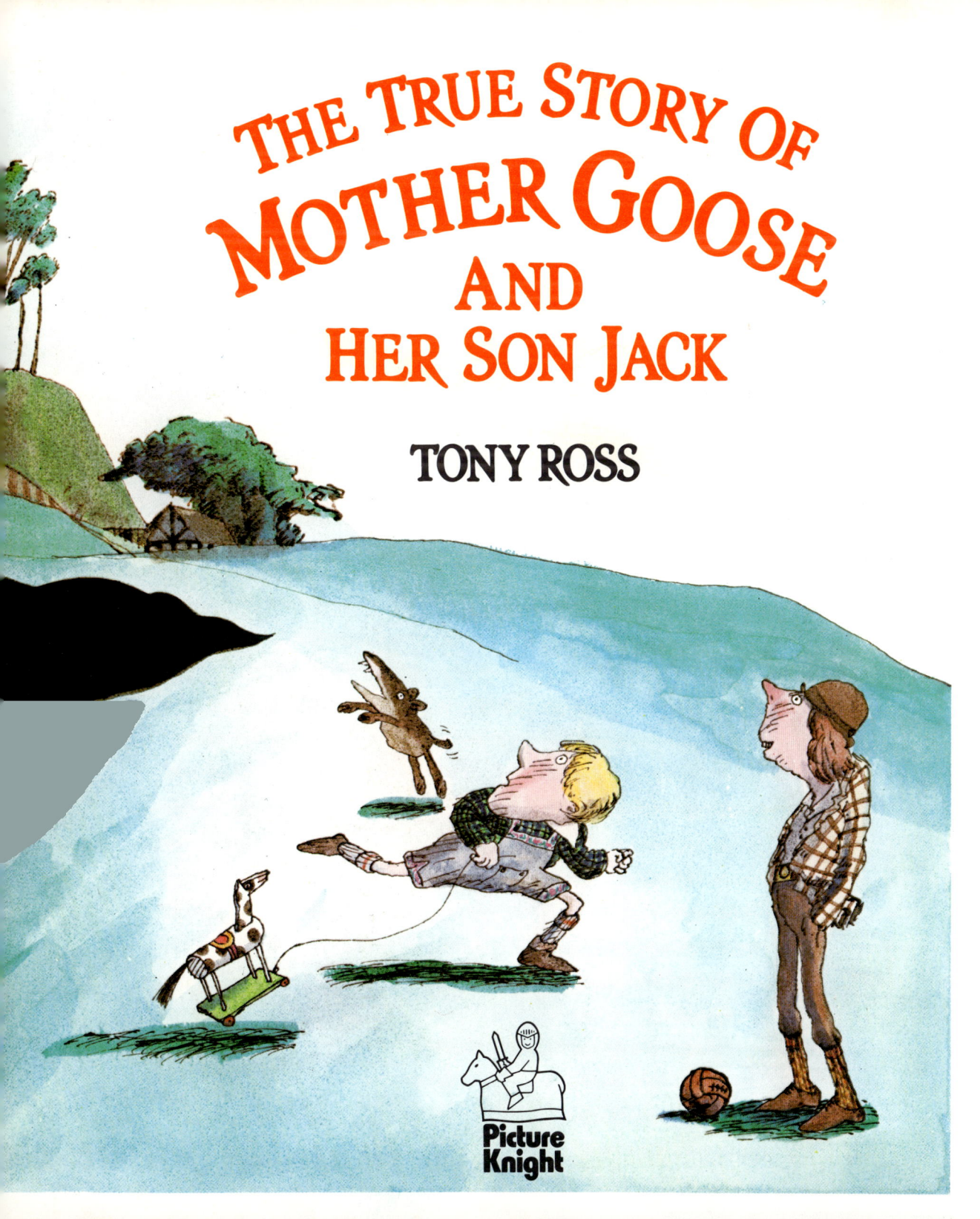

The True Story of Mother Goose and Her Son Jack

Tony Ross

Many years ago, a funny old woman lived on a funny old farm with her son, Jack.

They had no riches, no cows, and no horses. Nor had they any pigs, hens or goats. But they did have a fine gander.

As the gander was very big, and the old woman was quite small, she rode everywhere on its back. In this way, the shopping could be done without relying on public transport.

The old woman loved her gander.

Whenever they went dashing through the clouds, the townsfolk would rush out to watch and wave.

The children called her MOTHER GOOSE.

The gander soon became lonely and sad living by itself on the farm.

One day, Mother Goose (we will call her that too!) gave Jack some money.

"Go to the market," she said, "and buy a goose friend for the gander."

Dutifully, Jack set off, taking the clothes-prop with him, in case of trouble.

Once up on the high moor, Jack came across a huge robber, armed with fierce weapons. He was trying to wrench a pair of golden shoes off Maisie, the squire's daughter.

Jack had often admired the squire's daughter, so he decided to go to her rescue. Gripping the clothes-prop tightly, he stepped forward.

WHUNK! Jack brought the prop down on the robber's head.

The robber was so stunned and dazed that he ran away without looking at his assailant.

Maisie rushed over to thank Jack. When she heard that he was on his way to market, she whispered in his ear, "As a reward for your bravery, I'll give you a tip. At the market you will see an old woman selling geese. One of them, larger than the others, is extra special. Buy that one, and you'll not be sorry."

Maisie was gone in a twinkle of golden shoes.

At the market, Jack wandered about until he found the old goose seller. There was no mistaking the goose Maisie meant because it was so big.

"A handsome companion for the gander," he thought, handing over his money. "But how can it be *special*?"

Jack made his way home, holding the struggling goose, and puzzling over Maisie's words.

The gander and the goose liked each other at once, and everybody was happy. Jack told Mother Goose about Maisie's mysterious message, but even the old woman couldn't understand why the goose should be special.

The following morning, Jack was wakened by his mother's excited screeches. Rushing to see what the commotion was, he found her hopping from one foot to the other.

"A GOLDEN EGG, the goose has laid a GOLDEN EGG!"

Jack blinked at the huge shiny yellow egg, lying in the grass.

Jack set out for town at once.

As he was not used to selling golden eggs, he went into a tavern, to ask how to go about it. There he met a rogue who took the egg, and studied it carefully.

"There's not much call for these," whined the rogue, "but I'll do you a good turn, son. I'll take it off your hands for fifty shillings."

Although the egg was worth *much* more than that, Jack was dazzled by the amount, and snatched the money.

The rogue could hardly believe his good luck.

Mother Goose chased her son around the kitchen with a hairbrush, for his foolishness. Then she forgave him, and took him to the men's outfitters.

The fifty shillings was just enough for a new suit, a pair of fine boots, and a big hat covered in feathers.

"Now, my fine lad," she chuckled, "you can go and ask the squire for the hand of his daughter!"

Jack wriggled in his prickly new suit; he liked the idea of marrying Maisie.

"Thanks, Mum!" he said, and trotted off up the hill to the squire's house.

A footman presented Jack to a grumpy-looking man with a black beard and a blacker temper.

The lad bowed in a flutter of feathers.

"Sir," he said, "I would like to marry your beautiful daughter, Maisie, and ...."

Before he could finish, the squire and the footman took him by the arms, and marched him out into the garden.

At the bottom of the garden there was a horse trough. Without further ado, Jack was tossed into the slimy water.

"Impudent yokel!" sneered the squire. "A fifty-shilling suit doesn't make a gentleman!"

Unhappy Jack squelched off home to dry out in front of the fire. When Mother Goose had stopped laughing at his shrunken suit, she gave him another golden egg.

"Don't worry, son," she giggled, "the goose lays a golden egg every day. WE ARE RICH!"

And rich they became, as egg after egg was sold at a fair price.

News of the wonderful eggs travelled far and quickly. The squire wished he hadn't dunked Jack in the water, and the rogue wished that he had offered a fairer price, so that he could have other golden eggs.

Overcome with greed, he crept along to Jack's farm one black night, armed with a large carving knife. His plan was to cut open the goose, and steal any eggs still inside her. The rogue grabbed the goose, but she made so much noise she woke up the gander. The two birds squawked so loudly that Jack rushed out, and put the rogue to painful flight with the clothes-prop.

Jack's fame spread throughout the land, both for his wonderful goose, and for his bravery with the clothes-prop.

When he next visited the squire, it was a *very* different story. The squire was impressed by his fine appearance, and insisted he should walk in the garden with the beautiful Maisie.

They were married in June, and the squire (who was *much* nicer now) gave the happy couple a grand carriage and a white pony as a wedding present.

To the cheers of the townsfolk, Mr and Mrs Jack drove to their farm.

Mother Goose's present to the happy couple was the farm itself *and* the wonderful goose.

With kisses all round, she climbed on her gander, and disappeared into the clouds . . . forever.

She's still up there, somewhere, writing stories for children and posting them on the wind.

British Library Cataloguing in Publication Data

Ross, Tony
 The true story of Mother Goose and her son Jack.
 I. Title
 823'.914[J]   PZ8.1
 ISBN 0-340-42385-4

Copyright © Tony Ross 1979

First published 1979 by Andersen Press Ltd
This edition first published 1988 by Picture Knight

Published by Hodder and Stoughton Paperbacks,
a division of Hodder and Stoughton Ltd,
Mill Road, Dunton Green, Sevenoaks, Kent TN13 2YE
Editorial office: 47 Bedford Square, London WC1E 3DP

Printed in Great Britain by Cambus Litho,
East Kilbride

All rights reserved